NATURAL WONDERS OF THE WORLD

MOUNT EVEREST

by Lisa M. Bolt Simons

FOCUS READERS

FOCUS READERS

WWW.FOCUSREADERS.COM

Focus Readers is distributed by North Star Editions:
sales@northstareditions.com | 888-417-0195

Produced for Focus Readers by Red Line Editorial.

Content Consultant: Jeffrey R. Walker, PhD, Professor of Earth Science, Vassar College

Photographs ©: DanielPrudek/iStockphoto, cover, 1; Moroz Nataliya/Shutterstock Images, 4–5, 27; AP Images, 7; Daniel Prudek/Shutterstock Images, 9; Victor Josan/Shutterstock Images, 10–11; pawarit_s/Shutterstock Images, 12; Red Line Editorial, 15; Yongyut Kumsri/Shutterstock Images, 16–17; theskaman306/Shutterstock Images, 19; Efremova Irina/Shutterstock Images, 21; Pasang Geljen Sherpa/AP Images, 22–23; Malchev/iStockphoto, 25; Gurinder Osan/AP Images, 28–29

ISBN
978-1-63517-515-8 (hardcover)
978-1-63517-587-5 (paperback)
978-1-63517-731-2 (ebook pdf)
978-1-63517-659-9 (hosted ebook)

Library of Congress Control Number: 2017948093

Printed in the United States of America
Mankato, MN
November, 2017

ABOUT THE AUTHOR

Lisa M. Bolt Simons is a writer who has published more than 30 books with more on the way. She's also been a teacher for more than 20 years. Her fiction and nonfiction has been recognized with awards and grants. She lives in Minnesota.

TABLE OF CONTENTS

CHAPTER 1

THE HIGHEST MOUNTAIN IN THE WORLD

The peak rises from a mountain range known as the Himalayas. Ice boulders, crevices, and **glaciers** cover the mountain. Snow is always on the summit. The wind can blow more than 100 miles per hour (161 km/h). At 29,035 feet (8,850 m) above sea level, Mount Everest is the world's tallest mountain.

Snow, elevation, and cold conditions make Mount Everest one of Earth's most hostile places.

Mount Everest is on the border of Nepal and Tibet. In Tibet, the mountain is called Chomolungma. This name means "Goddess Mother of the World." In Nepal, Mount Everest is known as Sagarmatha.

IS IT REALLY THE TALLEST?

Mountains' elevations are usually listed from sea level. Mount Everest is the tallest using this method. But mountains can also be measured from the center of the earth. Using this method, Mount Chimborazo in Ecuador is the tallest. It is 1.5 miles (2.4 km) closer to outer space than Everest. Mauna Kea in Hawaii is also taller than Mount Everest when measured from its base at the ocean floor. However, more than half of Mauna Kea is under the sea.

In 1953, Edmund Hillary (left) and Tenzing Norgay became the first people to reach Mount Everest's summit.

In the Sanskrit language, this means "Peak of Heaven."

In English, the mountain was originally called Peak XV (fifteen). In 1865, it took on its current name. The mountain was named for Sir George Everest. He was a **surveyor** from the United Kingdom.

Each year, people attempt to climb Mount Everest. It is a long and dangerous journey. Most climbers need two months to reach the summit. They also need a lot of money. It can cost $20,000 just for a **permit** and insurance. This total does not include things such as guides, supplies, and food.

Faces, or surfaces, of Mount Everest join together to make ridges. Climbers walk on these ridges to reach the summit. Conditions on the mountain are harsh. In summer, the high temperature reaches about –2 degrees Fahrenheit (–19°C). In winter, temperatures are usually around –33 degrees Fahrenheit (–36°C). But if

Climbers hike toward Mount Everest's base camp.

a storm hits, the temperature can dive to –76 degrees Fahrenheit (–60°C). The weather can change quickly and unexpectedly on Mount Everest.

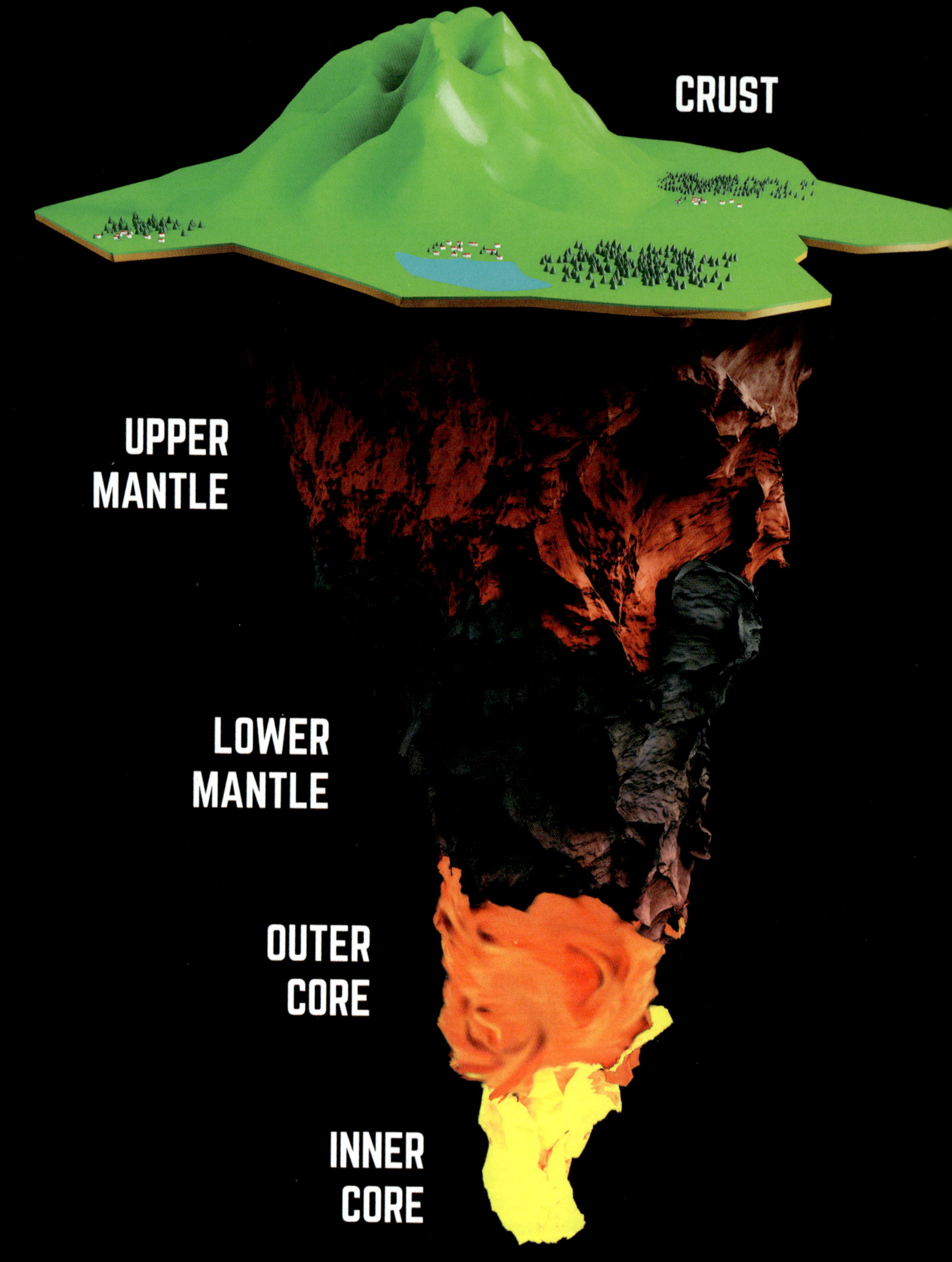
CRUST
UPPER MANTLE
LOWER MANTLE
OUTER CORE
INNER CORE

CHAPTER 2

MILLIONS UPON MILLIONS OF YEARS OLD

Earth is made up of layers. The two outer layers are the crust and the upper mantle. These layers are broken into 12 curved plates. The plates are always moving. The thickest plates are those under mountains. Approximately 40 to 50 million years ago, two of these plates crashed into each other.

The mantle is Earth's thickest layer at approximately 1,800 miles (2,900 km) thick.

The tallest mountains in the world are in the Himalayas.

This impact slowly created a mountain range. Around 25 million years later, it became the Himalayas. Mount Everest is one of the mountains in this range.

The Himalayas as we see them today began forming two million years ago. This process ended around 11,700 years ago. However, Mount Everest is still moving.

HOW TALL IS IT?

The measurements of Mount Everest have never been consistent. In 1856, explorers estimated the peak to be 29,002 feet (8,840 m) above sea level. In 1955, the government of India measured it at 29,029 feet (8,848 m). This height is still used in Nepal today. However, new technology has provided different measurements. The Global Positioning System (GPS) might provide a more accurate measurement. American and Chinese surveyors have used GPS. The Americans determined the mountain was 29,035 feet (8,850 m) tall. However, Nepal has not accepted the measurements.

It is inching to the northeast. It is also getting taller. However, the changes are small. The mountain grows approximately 0.16 inches (0.41 cm) taller each year.

Mount Everest has many different layers of rock. At the bottom are layers of gneiss and granite formed deep in the crust of the earth. Lying on top of these are beds of shales and mudstones formed at the bottom of a sea. Over these are limestone beds formed in a shallow sea. When plate impact closed the sea, these rocks were shoved high in the air. Near the top of Mount Everest, a visible formation of limestone and marble is called the Yellow Band.

INSIDE MOUNT EVEREST

Mount Everest looks as if it's made of rock and snow. However, several different layers of rock make up the mountain.

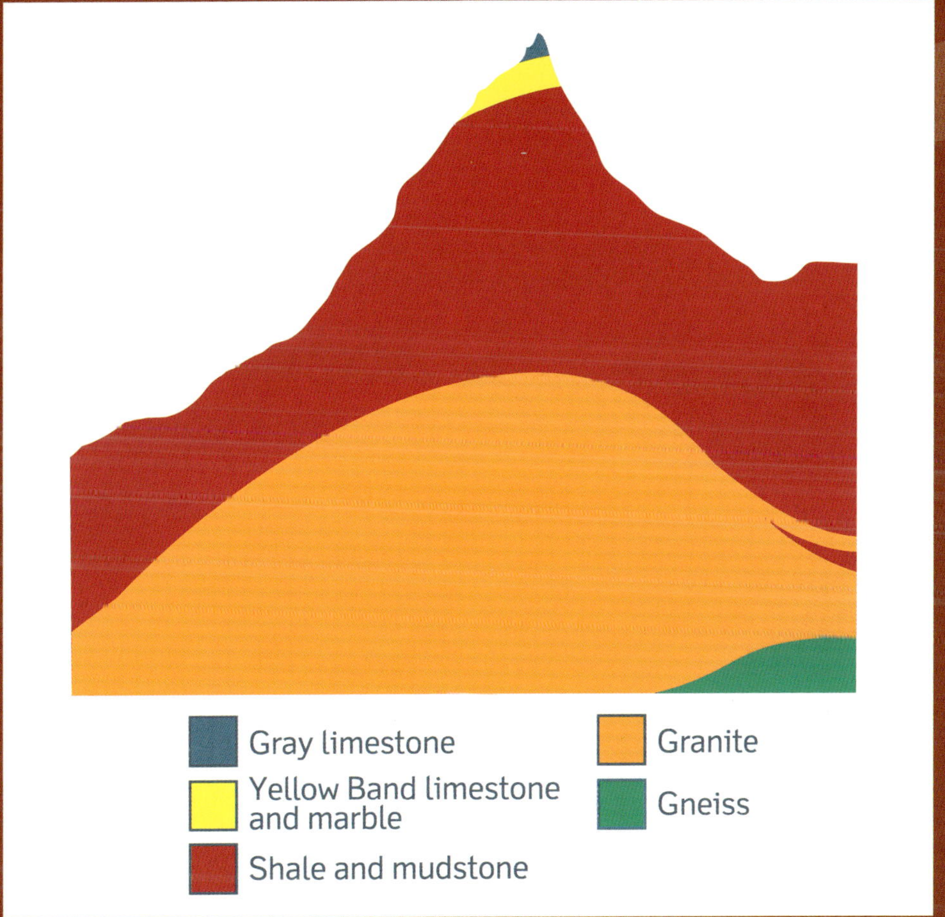

CHAPTER 3

TOO COLD FOR LIFE

The conditions atop Mount Everest are hostile. Microorganisms such as bacteria can survive at the summit. But there is less oxygen at high elevations. This makes it hard for animals to breathe. Temperatures are also very cold. These conditions prevent animals and plants from surviving atop the mountain.

There are different habitats among the elevations in the Himalayas.

However, several different animal species make their homes at lower elevations. These animals living on Mount Everest have developed **adaptations** for the climate. For example, snow leopards have developed wide paws and thick fur. These features help the animals live at high elevations. Snow leopards can be

AMAZING YAKS

Among mammals, the yak is best built for altitude. Yaks have two coats of fur. Their hearts and lungs are large. Enlarged organs are an adaptation for less oxygen. Plus, their bodies have **genes** that help them use energy from their food more **efficiently**, especially in the winter. These qualities allow yaks to climb up to 20,000 feet (6,096 m).

Yaks' adaptations allow them to climb high up Mount Everest.

found between 9,800 and 17,000 feet (2,987 and 5,182 m).

Some birds also survive at high altitudes. The snow partridge lives at 18,600 feet (5,669 m). During **migration**, bar-headed geese fly over the Himalayas at 23,000 feet (7,010 m).

Their adaptations include large lungs and a wide wingspan. The wingspan helps reduce the energy needed to fly.

The Himalayan jumping spider has been found at 22,000 feet (6,706 m). No animal on Earth lives higher. Bumblebees aren't far away, though. In 2008, a swarm of bees was found above 18,000 feet (5,486 m). No insect in the world lives higher than the bumblebee.

Plants cannot grow near the summit. But plenty grow lower on the mountain. A moss grows at 21,260 feet (6,480 m). It is the highest-growing plant in the world. Lower on the mountain, plants such as wildflowers grow in the meadows.

Plants have more opportunities to grow at lower elevations.

Farther down the mountain is scrubland. And lower in elevation are the **coniferous** forests. These are home to pine and fir trees. At the base of the Himalayas are the **deciduous** forests. Animals such as rhinoceroses, bears, and Asian elephants can be found here.

CHAPTER 4

STILL REACHING THE SUMMIT

The first successful climb to Mount Everest's summit was in 1953. Hundreds of people now climb the mountain each year. In fact, a record 371 climbers requested permits in 2017. Their journey is a difficult one.

There are various routes up the mountain. Most take the south route.

Climbers make their way up the Khumbu Icefall, a dangerous area between base camp and Camp 1.

First, climbers must hike to base camp. It is 17,500 feet (5,334 m) high. There are four smaller camps at higher elevations.

Climbers face many risks. Breathing becomes harder as they gain altitude. Extreme weather conditions can change in an instant. The climb itself includes many challenging sections, including rock climbing. Dozens of climbers have died on the mountain.

New technologies have helped climbers. They have better gear and weather forecasting. Expert guides also prepare the trails and help the climbers. These improvements have led to fewer deaths on the mountain since 2000.

THE SOUTH ROUTE

Most climbers take the south route up Mount Everest. On average, climbers need approximately two months to reach the summit.

These technologies have also made climbing the mountain more accessible. As more people climb, however, problems have arisen. Climbers bring many supplies, such as oxygen tanks. They often leave their trash on the mountain. Human waste is left on the mountain, too.

SHERPAS

The Sherpa people originally lived in villages up to 14,000 feet (4,267 m) high. In the early 1900s, foreign explorers needed help carrying supplies and surveying the land. Sherpas had adapted to the high altitude. They performed well. Sherpa guides still work on Mount Everest. However, people often refer to any local guide as a Sherpa.

People are working to protect Mount Everest for future generations.

New rules are helping. Now climbers must bring down some of their trash and waste.

Of course, Mount Everest will always battle the environment, too. The plates will keep shifting, and earthquakes will keep shaking. Time will tell what Mount Everest will look like thousands of years from now.

EXTRA OXYGEN

The Mount Everest summit has 66 percent less oxygen than there is at sea level. Not having enough oxygen affects sleep, the ability to digest food, and thinking. This presents a challenge for climbers who are already tested with the climb itself.

To adapt their bodies to less oxygen, climbers use a "climb high, sleep low" technique. They hike up to a camp during the day and then go down one camp to sleep. The camps are set up approximately 2,200 feet (671 m) apart in elevation. The south route has four camps between the base camp and the summit. Since the 1920s, most climbers have also used extra oxygen from tanks to make the journey safer.

A Sherpa guide carries used oxygen tanks. Climbers usually use extra oxygen starting at 25,000 feet (7,620 m).

FOCUS ON
MOUNT EVEREST

Write your answers on a separate piece of paper.

1. Write a sentence that describes what it's like to climb Mount Everest.

2. Would you ever want to climb Mount Everest? Why or why not?

3. What type of rock is found near Mount Everest's summit?

A. metamorphic
B. granite
C. limestone

4. What might have happened if animals had not adapted to the climate and altitude on Mount Everest?

A. The animals might have gotten tired.
B. The animals might have died.
C. The animals might have changed colors.

Answer key on page 32.

GLOSSARY

adaptations
Changes in an animal or its body parts that make it better suited to its environment.

coniferous
Relating to a type of tree that has needle-shaped leaves and produces cones.

deciduous
Relating to a type of tree that loses its leaves every year.

efficiently
Accomplishing as much as possible with as little effort or resources as possible.

genes
Chemical information in a living body.

glaciers
Large, slow-moving bodies of ice.

migration
When animals move to a different location, usually as the seasons change.

permit
A written form of permission by someone in charge.

surveyor
A person who studies and measures landforms.

TO LEARN MORE

BOOKS

Jankowski, Emily. *Reaching Everest's Summit*. New York: Gareth Stevens Publishing, 2015.

Lappi, Megan. *Mount Everest*. New York: AV2 by Weigl, 2013.

Medina, Nico. *Where Is Mount Everest?* New York: Penguin, 2015.

NOTE TO EDUCATORS

Visit **www.focusreaders.com** to find lesson plans, activities, links, and other resources related to this title.

INDEX

Answer Key: 1. Answers will vary; **2.** Answers will vary; **3.** C; **4.** B